The Essence of
Aristotle's
Nicomachean Ethics

The Essence of Aristotle's
Nicomachean Ethics

Edited by Hunter Lewis
and Stuart Kellogg

with an Introduction by
Hunter Lewis

Revised and updated version
of an original translation by
W. D. Ross

AXIOS

The Essence of . . . series of books are edited versions of great works of moral philosophy, distilled to reveal the essence of their authors' thought and argument. To read the complete, unedited version of this work, and see the excised passages, please visit our website at www.AxiosPress.com.

Axios Press
P.O. Box 118
Mount Jackson, VA 22842
888.542.9467   info@axiospress.com

Library of Congress Cataloging-in-Publication Data

    The essence of Aristotle's Nicomachean ethics / edited by Hunter
Lewis and Stuart Kellogg ; with an introduction by Hunter Lewis ; English translation by W. D. Ross.
      p. cm.
      Includes index.
      ISBN 978-1-60419-042-7 (pbk. : alk. paper)
      1. Aristotle. 2. Aristotle. Nicomachean ethics. 3. Ethics. I. Lewis,
Hunter. II. Kellogg, Stuart. III. Ross, W. D. (William David), 1877–1971.
IV. Aristotle. Nicomachean ethics. English.

B430.E85 2011

171'.3–dc22

                                                2010052406

Contents

Introduction

PEOPLE INFLUENCED BY Judaism and its related religions of Christianity and Islam tend to think of ethics as the study of right versus wrong. The ancient Greeks, including Aristotle, defined it instead as the study of the good versus the bad, a broader conception that incorporates right versus wrong but extends well beyond it.

The principal task of Aristotle's ethics is to define and illustrate the concept of *eudamonia*. This ancient Greek word has traditionally been translated as "happiness," but this is arguably misleading. In the text that follows, eudamonia is translated as "the best life," which is probably closer to what Aristotle meant. He was trying to think through the problem of how we should live and, by doing so, define the agathon "good" that we should be aiming for if we want "the best life."

Another key word for Aristotle is *arête*. This is usually translated as virtue. We have reluctantly kept this translation, but need to warn the reader that arête does not mean virtue in the same sense that we moderns often use that word. The problem once again arises from our tendency to view the world through the lens of Judaeo, Judaeo-Christian, or Judaeo-Islamic values.

In all these religions, virtue commonly refers to fixed rules of right and wrong. We are virtuous when we follow God's explicit (written) command and fall into vice when we do not. Aristotle's idea of arête is different. It can be translated as virtue, in the sense of a meritorious action, something in which we can take pride. It can also be translated as skill or mastery or an example of the highest practical intelligence.

Aristotle knew that the greatest Homeric heroes were thought by most ancient Greeks to exemplify arête, and Homeric heroes were certainly not always virtuous in a Christian or Muslim sense. So, as you read further about virtue and the virtues, please keep in mind that Aristotle is not describing saints, but rather people who are masterful in a worldly way.

Just to make this a little more complicated, there are times when Aristotle does speak of virtue and vice in the familiar voice of a quasi-Judaeo-preacher. For example, he condemns adultery in strong terms. But this is the exception. Usually the emphasis is on sorting out the good from the bad through reason and experience, not on following fixed moral rules.

Like most philosophers, Aristotle was a logician. Indeed, he is usually credited with the invention of formal logic. He relied on logic to arrive at his conclusions, and readers may feel that the logic occasionally gets lost in an overgrown thicket of verbal distinctions. The French philosopher Michel de Montaigne (1533–1592) deprecated this tendency of philosophy in his *Essays*:

> [The deductive method is all] preambles, definitions, classifications . . . etymologies [and] disputes . . . about words. . . . A stone is a body. But if you press the point: and what is a body?—a substance—and what is a substance? and so on. . . . One [merely] substitutes one word for another, that is . . . less well understood." [Such verbal gymnastics are followed by]:

> scattering and chopping . . . small questions [until] the world teem[s] . . . with uncertainties and disputes. . . . Have you ever seen [someone] trying to divide a mass of quicksilver into a number of parts? The more he presses and squeezes it, and tries to bring it under control, the more [it] keeps breaking and diversifying itself indefinitely. So it is here. . . . By the subdivision of these subtleties, we [accomplish little]. . . .

> Philosophy's object is to calm tempests
> of the souls, to teach . . . virtue, which
> does not, as the [logicians] allege, stand
> on the top of a sheer mountain, rugged
> and inaccessible. Those who have ap-
> proached it have found it, on the contrary,
> dwelling on a fair, fertile plateau, from
> which it can clearly see all things below
> it. . . . Anyone who knows the way can get
> there by shady, grassy, and sweetly flow-
> ering paths, pleasantly and up an easy and
> smooth incline. . . .*

Montaigne was an anti-logician, a pure empiricist who wanted to observe and study the world, find the best examples and practices, and learn from that. Aristotle was different; he was no anti-logician. Like all the followers of Socrates, he was excited by the prospect of using logic to reason through life's most perplexing questions. But, like Montaigne, Aristotle was also an empiricist, an observer, a collector of evidence, an organizer of observed facts, indeed one of the earliest empiricists.† As he said:

---

* Michel de Montaigne, *Essays*, translated by J. M. Cohen (London: Penguin Books, 1953), 67, 166, 346, 291.

† Who was the first empiricist in recorded history? Perhaps the Indian prince, Gautama, the Buddha, who was startlingly empiricist in his approach, and lived before Aristotle.

> We must consider our conclusion not only
> in terms of our premises, but also in light
> of further evidence. If a conclusion is true,
> all the data harmonize, but with a false one
> the facts soon clash.

Good empiricist that he was, he knew that any answers he developed about the nature of "the best life" would not be precise:

> It is the hallmark of an educated man to
> look for precision in a class of things only
> insofar as the nature of the subject admits.
> In other words, it is equally foolish to de-
> mand scientific proofs from a rhetorician as
> it is to settle for probable reasoning from a
> mathematician. And so we must be content
> to sketch the truth roughly and in outline.

Individuals would also have to use judgement in applying this truth both to themselves and to circumstances:

> That we must act according to the right
> rule is a common principle.... But we must
> agree that matters concerned with con-
> duct and questions of what is good for us
> have no fixity, no more than do matters
> of health. The agents themselves must in
> each case consider what is appropriate to

the occasion, just as in the arts of medicine and navigation.

Aristotle is not only an empiricist; he also has abundant common sense. For example, he stresses that it is not enough to identify "the best life." One must actually live it:

> At the Olympic Games, it is not the most beautiful or the strongest who are crowned, but those who compete, for it is from these the victors emerge. In the same way, it is necessary to act in order to win—rightly win—the noble and good things in life.

This common sense is not lofty. It is accompanied by a gritty realism:*

> We identify the best activities with the best life. But in order to engage in these best activities, we also require some external goods, as it is impossible, or at least not easy, to perform noble acts without the proper equipment. In many actions we rely on friends, riches, and political power as instruments; likewise, lacking certain things (e.g., good birth, good children, beauty) takes the luster from the best life.

---

* In the everyday, not the philosophical sense.

The man who is very ugly in appearance, ill born, or solitary and childless is unlikely to live the best life (this would be still less likely if he had thoroughly bad children or friends, or had lost good children or friends by death). The best life depends on a degree of prosperity.

Aristotle is not, however, a simple materialist in his interpretation of good living:

If great events turn out ill, they crush and maim the best life, bringing pain and hindering activities. Yet even in this case, nobility shines through when a man bears with resignation many great misfortunes, not because he is insensible to pain but through nobility and greatness of soul.

If, as we said, activities are what gives life its character, no man who seeks the best life can become completely miserable, for he will never commit acts that are hateful and mean. The man who is truly good and wise always makes the best of circumstances. This is so even should he suffer misfortunes like Priam's.*

---

* The king of ancient Troy whose city was sacked by the Greeks.

Lack of money or other material blessings can be a problem—nevertheless these are at best means to an end. What then is our end, our real purpose, as human beings seeking to live the best life? As Aristotle says:

> Wealth is evidently not the good we are seeking; it is merely useful and desired for the sake of something else. Pleasure, honor, and contemplation are more likely to be ends, since they are loved for themselves. But not even these are ultimate ends. . . .

> [An ultimate end] might be discovered if we could first ascertain the function of man. Have the carpenter and the tanner certain functions or activities, while men in general have none? Given that an eye, hand, foot—indeed, each of the body parts— evidently has a particular function, may one not reason that the whole man has a function apart from all these? If so, what can it be?

> We suggest that the unique function of man is to act, from the depths of his soul, in accord with a rational principle, which means in accord with virtue—or if there is more than one virtue, in accord with the best and most complete of these.

Aristotle then proceeds to define what virtue is and what the virtues are:

> Let us now examine the specific virtues, exploring what they are; what sort of things they are concerned with. . . .

> First, let us observe that right action is neither too little nor too much. For example, both excessive exercise and an utter lack of exercise destroy one's strength; similarly, consuming drink or food above or below a certain amount destroys the health, while that which is proportionate produces, increases, and preserves health. So too, in the case of temperance, courage, and the other virtues. The man who fears and flies from everything, not standing his ground against anything, becomes a coward. The man who fears nothing at all but goes to meet every danger becomes rash. Similarly, the man who indulges in every pleasure and abstains from none becomes self-indulgent, while the man who shuns every pleasure becomes ascetic. Both temperance and courage are preserved by the mean.

> Finding this mean requires effort. By abstaining from pleasures we become temperate,

and it is when we have become so that we are most able to abstain. Similarly in the case of courage, by being habituated to despise things that are terrible and to stand our ground against them, we become brave. And it is when we have become brave that we shall be most able to stand up to terrible things. . . .

We must also examine the things by which we ourselves are most easily carried away. Some of us tend to one thing, some to another; this is recognizable from the pleasure and pain we feel. We must drag ourselves toward the contrary extreme, for in order to achieve the intermediate state we must pull well away from error, as people do when straightening bent sticks. . . .

None of the moral virtues come to us by nature. If they did, we would have no choice about them. Neither by nature nor contrary to nature do the moral virtues arise in us; rather, we are adapted by nature to develop them, and they are made perfect by habit. . . . It makes no small difference whether we form habits of one kind or another from our very youth; indeed, it makes all the difference. . . .

Virtue is a manifestation of good character, which enables us to live well, just as good eyes enable us to see well. Good character reflects a mean, but not an arithmetic mean. For instance, if ten is many of something and two is few, six is the intermediate. Exceeding and exceeded by an equal amount, it is intermediate according to arithmetical proportion. But the intermediate relative to us is not so calculated. If ten pounds of food are too much for a particular person to eat and two too little, it does not follow that the trainer will order six pounds; for this may be too much for the person who is to take it, or too little—too little for the champion, too much for the beginning athlete.

Not every action or every passion admits of a mean. Some passions have names that already imply vice (e.g., spite, shamelessness, envy); and in the case of actions, adultery, theft, and murder. All of these suggest by their names that they are examples of vice, so that excesses or deficiencies do not apply to them. It is never possible to be right with regard to them; one must always be wrong. Nor is it better to commit adultery with the right woman, at the right time, and in the right way. Simply to do it is to go wrong....

The concept of the mean cannot be rigidly applied; in some cases the deficiency, in some cases the excess, is more opposed to the mean. For example, it is not rashness, which is an excess, but cowardice, which is a deficiency, that is more opposed to courage. Neither is it asceticism, which is a deficiency, but self-indulgence, which is an excess, that is more opposed to temperance. Since rashness is thought to be more similar to courage, and cowardice more unlike, we oppose the latter to courage; for things that are further from the intermediate are thought to be more contrary to it. In general, we describe as contrary to the mean the direction in which we, as humans, are more likely to go. Therefore self-indulgence, which is an excess, is rightly regarded as more contrary to temperance....

The passions that we possess are in themselves neither virtuous nor the opposite. By passions I mean appetite, anger, fear, confidence, envy, joy, friendly feeling, hatred, longing, emulation, pity—in general, the feelings that accompany pleasure or pain. A man is neither praised nor blamed for feeling anger but rather for *how* he feels anger. Also, we feel anger and fear without choice, but the virtues involve choice. The virtues, therefore, are not passions; nor are they the faculties through which we experience passions: They are, rather, manifestations of character. . . .

Most people, taking refuge in theory, imagine that they are philosophers and will become good "by thinking about it"; in this, they behave like patients who listen attentively to their doctors but follow through on none of the things prescribed for them. As the latter will not be made well in body by such a course of treatment, the former will not be made well in soul by such a course of philosophy.

So there we have it. The purpose of our life is to shape our character to reflect the virtues. If we do so, this will give us "the best life," unless some terrible calamity intervenes, and if it does, character will help us bear calamity with the least pain. This is both a highly idealistic and a highly realistic philosophy of life. It is not surprising that it should have held such a central place in both intellectual and moral history.

—Hunter Lewis

Biographical Sketch

ARISTOTLE (384–322 BCE) was born at Stagirus in northern Greece (Thrace). His father served as a physician to the King of Macedon, the grandfather of Alexander the Great, whom Aristotle would later tutor.

Following his father's death, the then 17-year-old Aristotle traveled to Athens where he became a pupil of Plato's. When Plato died in 347 BCE, Aristotle was not chosen to succeed him as head of the Academy, and accepted an invitation to transfer to Atarneus and Assos, where he married Pythias, niece of the King Hermeas. At some later point, Aristotle married again, this time to Herphyllis, who bore him a son Nicomachus, hence the title *Nicomachean Ethics*, a treatise addressed to his son.

After Hermeas was captured by the Persians through treachery and executed, Aristotle moved to

Mytilene, and then to Macedon, having accepted the invitation to tutor Alexander, then 13. After five years, the two must have become close, because Alexander sent him specimens to study as he traveled across Asia in his career of conquest. Once Alexander had embarked on his Kingship and military campaign, Aristotle returned to Athens where he set up his own school, the Lyceum. Because of Aristotle's habit of walking as he lectured, his followers were called Peripatetics.

The death of Alexander in 323 BCE brought an anti-Macedonian reaction in Athens. As part of this, Aristotle became endangered, and he chose to depart so that the Athenians would not sin twice against philosophy—a reference to the execution of Socrates. Not long after, in Chalcis, on the nearby island of Euboea, he died from a stomach complaint.

All of Aristotle's published work perished. Some of his unpublished work, including the *Nicomachean Ethics*, survived. This large trove of material, so original and groundbreaking, is nevertheless somewhat disorganized and repetitive. One idea is that it constitutes his lecture notes. Another idea is that it is notes jotted down by students as Aristotle taught. Even this material almost disappeared forever. It was preserved by Islamic scholars and republished in the 9th century. Eventually it was rediscovered in Europe and became immensely influential. Aristotle was equally a philosopher (including an economist) and early scientist, and remains one of the greatest minds of world history.

Book One

IT IS THE hallmark of an educated man to look for precision in a class of things only insofar as the nature of the subject admits. In other words, it is equally foolish to demand scientific proofs from a rhetorician as it is to settle for probable reasoning from a mathematician. And so we must be content to sketch the truth roughly and in outline.

The end of the medical art (that is, its goal) is health; that of shipbuilding, a vessel; that of military strategy, victory; that of economics, wealth. In each case, it is for the sake of the latter that the former is pursued.

Is there an end we desire for its own sake—desiring everything else for the sake of this? If so, it must be the chief good. And will not knowledge of it have a great influence on life? And shall we not, like archers who have a mark to aim at, be more likely to hit upon what is right? If so, we should try to determine what that end is.

The answer appears to be political life whose end must be the good for man. Even if the end is the same for a single man as for a state, that of the state seems to be greater and more complete: although it is worthwhile to attain the end for one man only, it is finer, more godlike, to attain it for a nation or for city-states. Our inquiry, therefore, leads us into the study of social and political life.

———— ⌘ ————

Given that all knowledge and every pursuit aim at some good, what does political study aim at, and what is the highest of all goods achievable by social and political action? The general run of men and people of superior refinement agree that it is the best life, and identify living well and doing well with living the best life. But men differ in their definition of "living and doing well." Many think it is attaining something obvious, such as pleasure, wealth, or honor. But often even the same man identifies the best life with different things: e.g., with health when he is ill, with wealth when he is poor.

———— ⌘ ————

Judging from the lives that men actually lead, the majority—and especially men of the most vulgar type—identify the best life with pleasure. On the other hand, people of superior refinement and active disposition identify the best life with honor, for that is, roughly speaking, the end of the political life. But this seems too superficial to be what we are seeking, since honor depends on those who bestow it. Furthermore, men seem to pursue honor in order that they may be assured of their own goodness. At least this is the case with men of practical wisdom, who regard virtue as superior to honor. One might even suppose that virtue, rather than honor, is the end of the political life. But this cannot be, since possession of virtue appears to be compatible with being asleep, with lifelong inactivity, and with the greatest suffering and misfortune; yet no one would claim that a man who lives in this way is living the best life.

After a lifetime spent in the pursuit of honor comes the contemplative life, but we shall consider that later.

Wealth is evidently not the good we are seeking; it is merely useful and desired for the sake of something else. Pleasure, honor, and contemplation are more likely to be ends, since they are loved for themselves. But not even these are ultimate ends.

———❧———

As there is more than one end, and we choose some of these (e.g., wealth) for the sake of something else, clearly not all ends are final ends; but the chief good is evidently something final. The best life is indeed something final and self-sufficient, and is the end of action. But to say that the best life is the chief good seems to be a platitude; a clearer account is still desired.

This might be discovered if we could first ascertain the function of man. Have the carpenter and the tanner certain functions or activities, while men in general have none? Given that an eye, hand, foot—indeed, each of the body parts—evidently has a particular function, may one not reason that the whole man has a function apart from all these? If so, what can it be?

We suggest that the unique function of man is to act, from the depths of his soul, in accord with a rational principle, which means in accord with virtue—or if there is more than one virtue, in accord with the best and most complete of these.

But we must add "in a complete life." One swallow does not make a summer, nor does one day; so, too, even a few years do not make a man blessed and cause him to live the best life.

Let this serve as an outline of the good—a first, rough sketch to be filled in later.

———— ⳹ ————

We must consider our conclusion not only in terms of our premises, but also in light of further evidence. If a conclusion is true, all the data harmonize, but with a false one the facts soon clash.

Our account is in harmony with those who identify the best life with virtue or with a single virtue, for to virtue belongs virtuous activity. But it matters a great deal whether we place the chief good in state of mind or in activity. At the Olympic Games, it is not the most beautiful or the strongest who are crowned, but those who compete, for it is from these the victors emerge. In the same way, it is necessary to act in order to win—rightly win—the noble and good things in life. We identify the best activities with the best life. But in order to engage in these best activities, we also require some external goods, as it is impossible, or at least not easy, to perform noble acts without the proper equipment. In many actions we rely on friends, riches, and political power as instruments; likewise, lacking certain things (e.g., good birth, good children, beauty) takes the luster from the best life. The man who is very ugly in appearance, ill born, or solitary and childless is unlikely to live the best life (this would be still less likely if he had thoroughly bad children or friends, or had lost good children or friends by death). The best life depends on a degree of prosperity.

It has been asked whether the best life is to be acquired by learning or by some kind of training, or does it come by divine providence or chance? The best life that is reached by a process of learning or training is the greatest thing in the world, something god-like and blessed. To entrust the most noble to chance would be a very defective arrangement.

Neither ox nor horse nor any other beast is living the best life, since none of them is capable of sharing in virtuous activity. For this reason also, a boy cannot live the best life, since owing to his age he is not yet capable of such acts. (Boys who are applauded for living the best life are being fussed over based on our hopes for their future.) As we said, to live the best life requires not only complete virtue but also a complete life, since many changes and chances occur over the course of years, and in old age even the most prosperous may fall into great misfortunes, as Homer tells of Priam in the Iliad. No one would describe as living the best life a man who has experienced such chances and ended up so wretched.

No function of man is as permanent as virtuous activity. He who lives the best life does so throughout his lifetime. By preference to everything else, he engages in virtuous action and contemplation, and will bear the chances of life most nobly and altogether decorously—but only if he is "truly good" and "beyond reproach."

Small pieces of good fortune or its opposite weigh little on the scales of life, but a multitude of great events—if they turn out well—can make life better.

Not only will they themselves add beauty to life, but the way a man deals with them may be noble and good. By contrast, if great events turn out ill, they crush and maim the best life, bringing pain and hindering activities. Yet even in this case, nobility shines through when a man bears with resignation many great misfortunes, not because he is insensible to pain but through nobility and greatness of soul.

If, as we said, activities are what gives life its character, no man who seeks the best life can become completely miserable, for he will never commit acts that are hateful and mean. The man who is truly good and wise always makes the best of circumstances. This is so even should he suffer misfortunes like Priam's.

Book Two

VIRTUE IS OF two kinds, intellectual and moral. Intellectual virtue owes both its birth and its development to teaching; for this reason it requires experience and time. Moral virtue comes from habit, whence its name *ethike*, formed by a slight variation from the word *ethos*.

None of the moral virtues come to us by nature. If they did, we would have no choice about them. Neither by nature nor contrary to nature do the moral virtues arise in us; rather, we are adapted by nature to develop them, and they are made perfect by habit.

We become just by doing just acts, temperate by doing temperate acts, brave by doing brave acts. This is confirmed by what happens in governments. Legislators make citizens good by fostering good habits in them. It is in this that a good constitution differs from a bad one.

It is from playing the lyre that lyre-players are produced. If this were not so, there would have been no need of a teacher; all men would have been born either accomplished or inept musicians (which clearly is not the case). The same is true of appetites and feelings of anger. By habitually behaving in one way or the other, some men become temperate and good-tempered, others self-indulgent and irascible. Therefore, it makes no small difference whether we form habits of one kind or another from our very youth; indeed, it makes all the difference.

The present inquiry does not aim at theoretical knowledge; we are not inquiring in order to know what virtue is but in order to become good. Therefore, we must examine the nature of actions—namely, how we ought to perform them—since these determine our character.

That we must act according to the right rule is a common principle and will be discussed later: both what the right rule is, and how it relates to the virtues. But first we must agree that matters concerned with conduct and questions of what is good for us have no fixity, no more than do matters of health. The agents themselves must in each case consider what is appropriate to the occasion, just as in the arts of medicine and navigation.

Although right action depends on the occasion, we must give what help we can. First, let us observe that right action is neither too little nor too much. For example, both excessive exercise and an utter lack of exercise destroy one's strength; similarly, consuming drink or food above or below a certain amount destroys the health, while that which is proportionate produces, increases, and preserves health. So, too, in the case of temperance, courage, and the other virtues. The man who fears and flies from everything, not standing his ground against anything, becomes a coward. The man who fears nothing at all but goes to meet every danger becomes rash. Similarly, the man who indulges in every pleasure and abstains from none becomes self-indulgent, while the man who shuns every pleasure becomes ascetic. Both temperance and courage are preserved by the mean.

Finding this mean requires effort. By abstaining from pleasures we become temperate, and it is when we have become so that we are most able to abstain. Similarly in the case of courage, by being habituated to despise things that are terrible and to stand our ground against them, we become brave. And it is when we have become brave that we shall be most able to stand up to terrible things.

———— ❧ ————

As we have seen, the virtues are concerned with actions and passions, and every action and every passion is accompanied by pleasure and pain. For this reason, virtue will be concerned with pleasures and pains.

It is on account of pleasure that we do bad things, and on account of pain that we abstain from noble ones. As Plato says, from our very youth we should have been brought up in a particular way so as to take pleasure in things we ought to take pleasure in or be pained by things we ought to be pained by.

There are three objects of choice (the noble, the advantageous, the pleasant) and three of avoidance, their contraries (the base, the injurious, the painful). The good man tends to go right and the bad man to go wrong especially about pleasure, which accompanies all objects of choice. Even the noble and the advantageous appear pleasant to us.

It is even harder to resist pleasure than anger, but every accomplishment, including virtue, is always concerned with what is harder. The man who uses pleasure and pain well will be good; he who uses them badly, bad.

———— ❧ ————

What makes an action good? Is it sufficient that it be good in outcome, regardless of intention? No. An agent of good must have knowledge. Secondly, he must choose the acts, and choose them for their own sakes. Thirdly, his action must proceed from a firm, unchangeable character.

It is by doing just acts the just man is produced; and by doing temperate acts, the temperate man. Without practicing and developing habits no one would have even a prospect of becoming good.

Most people, taking refuge in theory, imagine that they are philosophers and will become good "by thinking about it"; in this, they behave like patients who listen attentively to their doctors but follow through on none of the things prescribed for them. As the latter will not be made well in body by such a course of treatment, the former will not be made well in soul by such a course of philosophy.

───── ❧ ─────

The passions that we possess are in themselves neither virtuous nor the opposite. By passions I mean appetite, anger, fear, confidence, envy, joy, friendly feeling, hatred, longing, emulation, pity—in general, the feelings that accompany pleasure or pain. A man is neither praised nor blamed for feeling anger but rather for how he feels anger. Also, we feel anger and fear without choice, but the virtues involve choice. The virtues, therefore, are not passions; nor are they the faculties through which we experience passions: They are, rather, manifestations of character.

———— ❧ ————

Virtue is a manifestation of good character, which enables us to live well, just as good eyes enable us to see well. Good character reflects a mean, but not an arithmetic mean. For instance, if ten is many of something and two is few, six is the intermediate. Exceeding and exceeded by an equal amount, it is intermediate according to arithmetical proportion. But the intermediate relative to us is not so calculated. If ten pounds of food are too much for a particular person to eat and two too little, it does not follow that the trainer will order six pounds; for this may be too much for the person who is to take it, or too little—too little for the champion, too much for the beginning athlete.

Not every action or every passion admits of a mean. Some passions have names that already imply vice (e.g., spite, shamelessness, envy); and in the case of actions, adultery, theft, and murder. All of these suggest by their names that they are examples of vice, so that excesses or deficiencies do not apply to them. It is never possible to be right with regard to them; one must always be wrong. Nor is it better to commit adultery with the right woman, at the right time, and in the right way. Simply to do it is to go wrong.

———— ❧ ————

The concept of the mean cannot be rigidly applied; in some cases the deficiency, in some cases the excess, is more opposed to the mean. For example, it is not rashness, which is an excess, but cowardice, which is a deficiency, that is more opposed to courage. Neither is it asceticism, which is a deficiency, but self-indulgence, which is an excess, that is more opposed to temperance. Since rashness is thought to be more similar to courage, and cowardice more unlike, we oppose the latter to courage; for things that are further from the intermediate are thought to be more contrary to it. In general, we describe as contrary to the mean the direction in which we, as humans, are more likely to go. Therefore self-indulgence, which is an excess, is rightly regarded as more contrary to temperance.

———— ⌘ ————

It is not easy to be good; it is no easy task to find the middle. For example, it is easy to give or spend money; but to do this to the right person, to the right extent, at the right time, with the right motive, and in the right way—that is not easy. Goodness is noble, laudable, and rare.

We must also examine the things by which we ourselves are most easily carried away. Some of us tend to one thing, some to another; this is recognizable from the pleasure and pain we feel. We must drag ourselves toward the contrary extreme, for in order to achieve the intermediate state we must pull well away from error, as people do when straightening bent sticks.

As we have said, this is difficult, and especially in individual cases. It is not easy to determine how, with whom, on what provocation, and for how long we should be angry. We sometimes praise those who fall short of the mean and wrongly call them good-tempered. Sometimes we praise those who get too angry—or angry for too long—and call them manly. Deviating a little from goodness is not blamed, whether we do so in the direction of the more or of the less. But if we deviate more widely, this does not fail to be noticed. Up to what point and to what extent must a man deviate before he becomes blame-worthy? This is not easy to determine by reasoning, no more than anything else perceived by the senses. Such things always depend on particular facts and on our perception of the facts.

Book Three

PRAISE OR BLAME is bestowed on voluntary passions and actions; on those that are involuntary, we bestow pardon and sometimes also pity. To distinguish the voluntary from the involuntary is necessary for those who are studying the nature of virtue.

Those things thought involuntary take place under compulsion or owing to ignorance. When something is done from fear of a greater evil or for some noble object—e.g., if a tyrant, having your parents and children in his power, were to order you to do something base, promising that if you commit the act your family will be saved, but otherwise they will be put to death—it may be debated whether such actions are involuntary or voluntary. Such deeds, though mixed, are more like voluntary actions, for they are worthy of choice at the time they are done, and the end of an action is relative to the occasion.

For such mixed actions, men are sometimes even praised: for example, when they endure something base or painful in order to gain great and noble objects. On some actions praise is not bestowed, but pardon is: e.g., when a man does what he ought not, being under a pressure that overstrains human nature and which no one could withstand.

Some acts, perhaps, we cannot be forced to do; we ought rather to face death after the most fearful sufferings. Granted, it is sometimes difficult to determine what should be chosen and at what cost, and what should be endured in return for what gain. It is even more difficult to abide by our decisions.

The man who does something owing to ignorance and is not the least troubled by his action, has not acted voluntarily, since he did not know what he was doing; neither has he acted involuntarily, since he is not pained. Those who act by reason of ignorance but who repent may be considered involuntary agents. But those who do not repent are different; we might call them "non-voluntary agents." Since they differ from the other, it is better that they should have a name of their own.

Acts done by reason of anger or appetite are not rightly called involuntary. It would be odd to describe as involuntary the things one ought to desire; and we ought both to be angry at certain things and to have an appetite for other things: e.g., for health and for learning.

The irrational passions are no less human than reason is.

———— ❧ ————

Choice seems to be voluntary, but involves more than being voluntary; the latter extends more widely. Both children and the lower animals share in voluntary action but not in choice; therefore, we describe acts done on the spur of the moment as voluntary, but not as chosen.

We share appetite and anger with irrational creatures, but we do not share choice with them. The incontinent man acts with appetite but not with choice; the continent man, on the other hand, acts with choice but not with appetite.

Just as choice differs fundamentally from both appetite and anger, so, too, does it differ from desire or wish. A wish may relate to things that could never be brought about by one's own efforts: e.g., that a particular actor or athlete win in a competition. In addition, a wish relates to the end, choice to the means. Thus, we wish to be healthy, but we choose to engage in those activities which will make us healthy. In general, choice seems to relate to the means that are in our own power.

Choice must not be confused with opinion. The latter is distinguished by its falsity or truth, not by its badness or goodness; choice is distinguished by these. By choosing what is good or bad, we become men of a certain character, something that does not result simply from holding certain opinions.

No one encourages us to do things that are neither in our power nor voluntary; it is assumed that there is no gain in being persuaded not to be hot, in pain, hungry, etc., since we shall experience these feelings in any case.

It is in our power to do noble or base acts, and likewise in our power not to do them; this is what is meant by being good or bad. Likewise it is in our power to be either virtuous or vicious.

It is for this reason that legislators punish those who commit wicked acts (unless they have acted under compulsion or as the result of an ignorance for which they are not themselves responsible). Likewise, legislators honor those who do noble acts.

We may punish a man for his ignorance if he is deemed responsible for the ignorance: for example, when penalties are doubled in the case of drunkenness, since the man himself had the power not to get drunk, and his being drunk was the source of his ignorance. We also punish those who are ignorant of a law that they ought to know and is not difficult to grasp. So, too, in the case of anything else that they are thought to be ignorant of through carelessness; we assume that it is in their power not to be ignorant, since they have the power of taking care.

Perhaps a man is of the sort who do not take care, who live slack lives; they are responsible for becoming that way. Men make themselves responsible for being unjust or self-indulgent: in the first case by cheating, in the other by spending their time in drinking bouts and the like. Focusing on certain activities, be they vicious or praiseworthy, forms the corresponding character (this is seen in the case of people training for any contest or action; they practice the activity all the time). Not to know that it is by devoting one's actions to particular objects that states of character are produced is the sign of a thoroughly senseless person. It is irrational to suppose that a man who acts unjustly does not wish to be unjust or a man who acts self-indulgently does not intend to be self-indulgent. Yet it does not follow that if he wishes, he will cease to be unjust and will be just. A man who is ill does not become well by wishing to be well. As with illness, actions are required, and there may or may not be sufficient time.

No one blames those who are ugly by nature; we blame those who are ugly owing to want of exercise and care. So it is with respect to weakness and infirmity: no one would reproach a man sightless from birth or blinded by disease or from a blow; we would rather pity him. But everyone would blame a man who was blinded by wine or some other form of self-indulgence.

With regard to the virtues in general, we have argued that they are means; that they are aspects of character; that they tend, by their own nature, to produce the acts by which they are in turn further produced; and that they are in our power and voluntarily chosen. Let us now examine the specific virtues, exploring what they are, what sort of things they are concerned with, and how they are concerned with them.

Let us first speak of courage.

———— ❧ ————

That courage is a mean between feelings of fear and overconfidence has already been shown.

We fear all evils (disgrace, poverty, disease, friendlessness, death, etc.), but the brave man is not equally concerned about all of them. Perhaps we ought not to fear poverty and disease, nor, in general, the things that do not proceed from vice or are not due to our own action. Yet not even he who is unafraid of these is truly brave.

With what sort of terrible things is the brave man concerned? Surely with the greatest, for no one is more likely than he to stand his ground against the horrific. Of all things, death is the most terrible; it is the finale, and nothing is thought to be either good or bad for the dead. But the brave man is not concerned about death in all circumstances, e.g., at sea or in disease. In what circumstances, then? Surely in the noblest, death in battle; for this takes place amid the greatest and noblest danger. Deaths in battle are correspondingly honored in city-states and at the courts of monarchs. Quite properly, he is called brave who is fearless in the face of a noble death; and of all emergencies involving the likelihood of dying, the emergencies of war are in the highest degree of this kind.

Not all men find the same things terrible.

We say there are things terrible even beyond human strength; these, then, are terrible to every one, at least to every sensible man; but the terrible things that are not beyond human strength differ in magnitude and degree, and so, too, do the things that inspire confidence. The brave man is as dauntless as man can be. Though he will fear even things that are not beyond human strength, he will face them as he ought and as the rule directs, for honor's sake; for this is the end of virtue. But it is possible to fear these more, or less, and to fear things that are not terrible as if they were. Of the faults that are committed, one consists of fearing what one should not, another in fearing as we should not, another in fearing when we should not, and so on. So, too, with respect to the things that inspire confidence. The man who fears and faces the right things and from the right motive, in the right way and from the right time, and who feels confidence under the corresponding conditions, is brave; for the brave man feels and acts according to the merits of the case and in whatever way the rule directs. The end of every activity should conform to the highest state of character. This is true, therefore, of the brave man as well as of others.

Courage is noble. To pursue an end of courage is therefore also noble. It is for a noble end that the brave man endures and acts as courage directs.

Rash men are precipitate, wishing for dangers beforehand but drawing back when they are in them. Brave men, on the other hand, are keen in the moment of action but quiet beforehand. The coward, the rash man, and the brave man, therefore, are concerned with the same objects but are differently disposed towards them: the first two exceed and fall short, while the third holds the middle (i.e., the right) position.

Though courage is concerned with both feelings of overconfidence and of fear, it is not concerned with both alike, but more with fear. Fear is painful, and it is for facing what is painful that men are called brave—just praise, indeed, for it is harder to face what is painful than to abstain from what is pleasant.

The end that courage sets before itself could actually be described as pleasant, but a pleasure concealed by the attending circumstances. This is true also of athletic contests. The end at which boxers aim—the crown and the honors—is pleasant although the blows they take are painful and distressing to flesh and blood, as is the whole exertion. The case of courage is similar; wounds and death are painful to the brave man and suffered against his will, but he faces them because it is noble to do so or because it is base not to do so. The more he is possessed of virtue in its entirety and the happier he is, the more he will be pained by thoughts of death; for life is best worth living for such a man, and he is knowingly at risk of losing the greatest of goods. This is painful, but he is brave nonetheless; perhaps all the more so, because he chooses noble deeds of war and accepts the cost.

So much, then, for courage. It is not difficult to grasp its nature in outline.

Now let us speak of temperance.

We have said that temperance is a mean with regard to pleasure (it is less concerned with pain). Let us now determine with what sort of pleasure it is concerned.

We may begin with a distinction between bodily pleasures and those of the soul, such as love of honor and love of learning. Men who are concerned with the last-mentioned are called neither temperate nor self-indulgent. Neither are those who are concerned with other pleasures that are not physical. Those who are fond of hearing and telling stories, wasting their days on rumor mongering, are called gossips, but are not called self-indulgent.

Temperance is concerned with physical pleasures, but not with all of these. Those who delight in objects of vision, such as colors and shapes and painting, are called neither temperate nor self-indulgent. It is the same with objects of hearing: no one reproaches those who delight extravagantly in music or the drama for being self-indulgent. Nor do we praise those who delight in music less for being temperate. Likewise, we do not call those self-indulgent who delight in the fragrance of apples, roses, or incense.

Temperance and self-indulgence do apply to the kind of pleasures that the other animals share in; these pleasures can appear slavish and brutish, especially touch and taste. But even taste is of less account; for the business of taste is to discriminate among flavors. Professional wine tasters and people who season dishes hardly take pleasure in their discriminations. In all cases, the actual enjoyment comes through touch or contact, whether in the case of food or drink or sexual intercourse. To delight in such things, and to love them above all others, puts us on a level with animals. The most self-indulgent are scarcely moved by the best pleasures of touch (those produced in the gymnasium by massage and by the consequent heat), for the contact such people seek does not affect the whole body but only certain parts of it.

—◆—

Some appetites seem to be common, others to be peculiar to individuals and acquired. The appetite for food is natural, since anyone who lacks them craves food or drink. So, too, is the appetite for sex among the young. In the natural appetites few go wrong, and then in only one direction, that of excess. To consume until one is surfeited is to exceed the natural amount, which is why people who overindulge in food and drink are called belly-gods. To fill one's belly beyond what is right is a sign of slavish character.

The self-indulgent man, then, craves all pleasant things or those that are most pleasant, and is led by his appetite to choose these at the cost of everything else; therefore, he is pained when he fails to get them and even when he is merely craving them. It seems absurd to be pained for the sake of pleasure.

The temperate man occupies a middle position with regard to these objects. He neither enjoys the things the self-indulgent man enjoys most (rather, he dislikes them). Nor does he feel pain or craving when they are absent—or does so to a moderate degree, and not more than he should, nor when he should not, and so on. The things that are both pleasant and conducive to health or physical fitness, he will desire moderately; also other pleasant things if they are not hindrances to these ends, or contrary to what is noble, or beyond his means. In short, he does not love such pleasures more than they are worth.

Self-indulgence is a more voluntary state than cowardice. Therefore, it is more a matter of reproach. The self-indulgent man is subject to craving and desire, although no one craves to be self-indulgent.

Self-indulgence often seems childish. After all, children live at the beck and call of appetite, and it is in them that the craving for what is pleasant is strongest. Among adults, the desire for pleasure, if not obedient to a ruling principle, becomes insatiable even if gratified; the exercise of appetite just increases its innate force. Appetites so strong and violent may even expel the power of calculation; therefore, they must be kept in check. Just as the child should live according to the direction of his tutor, so the appetitive element should be governed by reason. The rational and temperate man desires the things he ought, as he ought, when he ought.

Book Four

LET US NOW speak of appropriate spending, which describes a mean between the miser and the prodigal spender, and especially between the miser and the generous, discriminating giver. Riches will be employed best by the man who finds this middle point. He, who does so and is generous, is often the most loved of men.

The truly generous man, like other virtuous men, gives for the sake of the noble. He will give to the right people, in the right amounts, and at the right time, and he will do so with pleasure or without pain; for that which is virtuous is pleasant or free from pain—least of all will it be painful. But he, who gives to the wrong people or not for the sake of the noble but rather for some other cause, cannot be called generous. Nor is he generous who gives with pain; he prefers wealth to the noble act.

The generous man does not acquire goods or money from tainted sources (a sure sign of setting too much store by wealth). Nor will he be a ready asker; a man who confers benefits ought not to accept them lightly from others. Nor will he neglect his own property, since he depends on it in order to help others. And he will refrain from heedlessly giving to anybody and everybody, lest he have nothing left over to give to the right people, at the right time, and where it is noble to do so. And yet, it is highly characteristic of a generous man to go too far in giving, so that he leaves too little for himself; it is his nature not to look to himself.

Before calling a man "generous," we must have some idea of his wealth or lack thereof. Generosity is relative and resides not in the multitude of gifts but in the state of the giver's finances. There is nothing to prevent the man who gives less from being the more generous man.

It is not easy for the generous man to be rich, since he does not value wealth for its own sake but instead as a means of giving to others. No one can have wealth if he does not take pains to acquire and preserve it.

The man we have in mind governs both his giving and taking of wealth. He will both give and spend the right amounts and on the right objects, alike in small things and in great, and that with pleasure; he will also take the right amounts and from the right sources. Proper taking and giving are present together in the same man, while the contrary modes of miserliness and prodigality are not.

Prodigal behavior cannot last long, for it is not easy to spend and give to everybody if you take from none. (The prodigal, who soon exhausts his substance, is not thought wicked or ignoble, only foolish.)

Prodigal people also take from the wrong sources. Why? Because they wish to spend but their coffers are soon depleted. Caring nothing for honor, they take recklessly and from any source. Their giving is also inappropriate: it is not noble and does not aim at nobility, nor is it done in the right way. Sometimes the prodigal enriches those who should be poor, gives nothing to people of respectable character and showers gifts on flatterers or those who provide some other pleasure.

Treated with care, the prodigal man will arrive at the intermediate state, the right state. But the miser is incurable; his condition is more deeply rooted in human nature.

Some individuals err by taking anything from any source, even from those who ply disreputable trades: e.g., usurers, robbers, those who engage in fraud, and others who share a sordid love of gain. They put up with a bad name for the sake of gain, and little gain at that. Those who make great gains but from wrong sources—e.g., despots when they sack cities and spoil temples—we do not call mean but rather wicked, impious, and unjust.

We now should discuss appropriate living on a large scale. This also seems to be a virtue involving wealth; but unlike liberality, it does not extend to all the actions that are concerned with wealth, only to those that involving expenditure; and in these it surpasses liberality in scale. The scale is relative: the expense of equipping a trireme is not the same as that of heading a sacred embassy.

We are not describing the man who in small or middling ways spends according to the merits of the case, but rather one who spends appropriately on a magnificent scale. This virtue lies between, on the one hand, a refusal to spend when appropriate and, on the other hand, vulgar displays of wealth. The appropriately magnificent man is like an artist; he can see what is fitting and spends large sums tastefully.

The result should be worthy of the expense, and the expense should be worthy of the result—or should even exceed it. The appropriately magnificent man will spend such sums for honor's sake and will do so gladly, without close reckoning. He will consider how the result can be made most beautiful and most becoming, rather than how it can be produced most cheaply.

A poor man cannot be magnificent, since he lacks the means with which to spend large sums fittingly. He who tries to do so is a fool, since he spends beyond what can be expected of him and, therefore, more than what is proper. But great expenditure is becoming to those who have suitable means at the start, wealth acquired by their own efforts or inherited from ancestors. It brings them greatness and prestige. The magnificent man does not spend on himself but on public objects; in this, his gifts bear some resemblance to votive offerings. A magnificent man will also furnish his house in a manner commensurate with his wealth (for even a house is a sort of public ornament). He also prefers to spend on works that are lasting, as these are the most beautiful.

Such, then, is the appropriately magnificent man. The vulgar man, by contrast, succumbs to excess and spends beyond what is right. He spends too much on small objects and displays a tasteless showiness. For example, he hosts a club dinner on the scale of a wedding banquet, and when he provides the chorus for a comedy, he brings it onstage garbed in purple, as they do at Megara. All such things he does not for honor's sake but to show off his wealth, and because he thinks he can buy admiration. Where he ought to spend much, he spends little, and where little, much. The grasping and calculating man, on the other hand, falls short in everything. After spending the greatest sums, he will spoil the beauty of the result for the sake of a trifling economy; and in whatever he is doing, he hesitates and considers how he might spend less.

Great self-confidence, appropriate pride in one's ability—these must be directed to great things. A man is thought to be appropriately proud who, being worthy of them, thinks himself worthy of great things. He who does so beyond his deserts is a fool, and no virtuous man is foolish or silly. He who is worthy of little, and thinks himself worthy of little, is not proud. Pride implies largeness, as beauty implies a good-sized body (little people may be neat and well proportioned but cannot be beautiful). On the other hand, he who thinks himself worthy of great things but is in fact unworthy of them is vain. The man who regards himself as less worthy than he really is may be called unduly humble, whether his deserts be great or moderate.

The appropriately proud man, then, is an extreme with respect to the greatness of his claims, but a mean with respect to their rightness. If, then, he claims and deserves great things, he will be concerned with one thing in particular: honor, the prize appointed for the noblest deeds and surely the greatest of external goods.

To be appropriately proud, a man must be good in the highest degree. The better man always deserves more, and the best man most. Greatness in every virtue would seem to be expected of such a man. It would be most unbecoming for him to fly from danger, swinging his arms by his sides, or to wrong another; for to what end should he do disgraceful acts? If we consider him point by point, we see the utter absurdity of a proud man who is not good. Nor, again, would he be worthy of honor if he were bad. Honor is the prize of virtue, and it is to the good that it is rendered. Appropriate pride, then, seems to be a sort of crown of the virtues; it makes them greater and is not found without them. It is difficult to attain appropriate pride, for it is impossible without true nobility and goodness of character.

In the first place, as has been said, the appropriately proud man is concerned with honors. Yet he will bear himself with moderation toward wealth and power and all good or evil fortune, whatever may befall him, and will be neither overjoyed by good fortune nor overly troubled by evil. Not even when contemplating honor does he bear himself as if it were a very great thing. For him to whom even honor is minor, all else must be too; hence proud men are thought to be disdainful.

Men who are well born are thought worthy of honor, as are those who enjoy power or wealth. They are in a superior position, and everything that is superior in something good is held in greater honor. But in truth only the good man is to be honored. Those who, without virtue, possess power or riches are neither justified in making great claims nor entitled to be called proud: disdainful and insolent, but not proud;

for without virtue it is not easy to bear good fortune gracefully, and thinking themselves superior to others, they despise others and do whatever they please. They imitate the virtuous proud man without being like him.

The appropriately proud man does not chase trifling dangers, nor is he fond of danger. But he will face great dangers, and when he is in peril is unsparing of his life, knowing that there are situations in which life is not worth having. He is the sort of man to confer benefits but is ashamed of receiving them, for the one is the mark of a superior, the other of an inferior.

It is a mark of the proud man to ask for nothing (or scarcely anything) but to give help readily; to be dignified with people who enjoy high position and good fortune, but unassuming towards those of the middle class. It is a difficult and lofty thing to be superior to the former, but easy to be so to the latter. A lofty bearing with the great is no mark of ill breeding, but among humble people it is as vulgar as a display of strength against the weak.

Again, it is characteristic of the proud man to aim neither at the things commonly held in honor nor the things at which others excel; to hold back except where great honor or a great work is at stake; to be a man of few deeds, but these great and notable. Furthermore, he must be open in his hate and in his love, since to conceal one's feelings, to care less for truth than for what people will think, is a coward's part. He tells the truth, except when he speaks in irony to the vulgar.

He is unable to make his life revolve around another (unless it be a friend), for this is slavish; it is people lacking in self-respect who are flatterers. Nor is he given to admiration, since to him nothing is great. Nor is he mindful of wrongs; it is not characteristic of a proud man to have a long memory, especially for wrongs, but rather to overlook them. He does not gossip; he will speak neither about himself nor about another. In keeping with a character sufficient to itself, he will choose to possess beautiful and profitless things rather than the profitable and useful.

A slow step, a deep voice, and a level utterance are thought proper to the proud man. A shrill voice and a rapid gait stem from hurry and excitement, but the man who takes few things seriously is unlikely to be hurried or excited.

Such, then, is the proud man who deserves to be proud. The man who falls short of him is unduly humble; the man who goes beyond him is vain. These are not thought to be bad (they are not malicious), but only mistaken. The unduly humble man, being worthy of good things, robs himself of what he deserves; he also seems not to know himself. Yet such people are not thought to be fools but rather as unduly retiring. Vain people, on the other hand, are manifestly fools and ignorant of themselves. They attempt honorable undertakings and are soon found out. They adorn themselves with fine clothing and outward show; and wishing their strokes of good fortune to be made public, they speak about them as if they deserved to be honored for lucky chance. But undue humility is actually more opposed to pride than is vanity, for it is both a graver fault and more common.

———— ⁂ ————

In the sphere of honor, there appears to be another virtue besides appropriate pride, a mean with respect to honor that is not on the grand scale.

Just as expenditure may be too little or too much, honor may be desired more or less than is right. We blame both the ambitious man for seeking honor more than is right and from wrong sources, and the unambitious man for being unwilling to be honored even for noble reasons. Sometimes we praise the ambitious man as being manly and a lover of what is noble, and the unambitious man as being moderate and self-controlled. Evidently, we do not always assign the term "ambition" (i.e., "love of honor") to the same thing. When we praise the quality, we think of the man who loves honor more than do most people; when we blame it, we think of him who loves honor excessively. The mean being without a name, the extremes seem to dispute for its place. But where there is excess and defect, there is also an intermediate. This is the state of character that is praised, an unnamed mean with respect of honor. Relative to ambition, it seems to be lack of ambition; relative to lack of ambition, it seems to be ambition. In this case the extremes seem to be contradictory because the mean has not received a name.

The man who is angry at the right things and at the right people—as he ought, when he ought, and as long as he ought—deserves praise. This is the good-tempered man, he who tends to be unperturbed, erring rather in the direction of a deficiency of anger. He is not revengeful, instead making allowances.

At the same time, those who are not angry at the things they should be angry at are considered fools unlikely to defend themselves. To endure being insulted or put up with one's friends' being insulted is slavish.

At the other extreme, hot-tempered people get angry quickly, with the wrong persons, at the wrong things, and more than is right. They do not restrain their anger but retaliate openly owing to their quickness of temper. But their anger ceases quickly—which is the best point about them. Sulky people, by contrast, are hard to appease; they retain their anger because they repress it. Their anger ceases once they retaliate, for revenge relieves them of their rage, producing pleasure instead of pain. In the absence of retaliation, they hoard their burden of hurt. Such people are most troublesome to themselves and to their dearest friends.

Bad-tempered people are more common than those deficient in anger and more difficult to live with.

As we have said before in reference to other virtues and vices, it is not easy to define how, with whom, at what, and for how long one should be angry: that is, at what point right action ceases and wrong begins. The man who strays a little from the path, either toward the more or toward the less, is not blamed. Sometimes we praise those who exhibit the deficiency, and call them good-tempered; sometimes we call angry people manly and capable of ruling. How far a man must stray before he becomes blameworthy is not easy to say; the decision depends on the particular facts and also on perception. But this much at least is plain, that we must cling to the middle state.

Some men are thought to be obsequious, namely, those who praise everyone and everything and never oppose. Those of a contrary type are labeled contentious. The man who corresponds to the middle state is very much what, with affection added, we call a good friend. He associates with people in the right way, behaving differently with people in high station and with ordinary people, with closer and more distant acquaintances, and rendering to each class what is fitting.

The boastful man is apt to claim the things that bring glory when he has not got them, or to claim more of them than he has. The mock-modest man, on the other hand, denies what he has or belittles it. But the man who observes the mean is one who calls a thing by its own name, being truthful both in life and in word, and owning to what he has—neither more nor less.

Life includes rest as well as activity, and in rest are included leisure and amusement. Those who, seeking amusement, carry humor to excess are thought to be vulgar buffoons, striving after humor at all costs, and aiming to raise a laugh rather than saying what is becoming. They make no effort to avoid hurting the butt of their jokes. Those who can neither make a joke themselves nor put up with those who can, are thought to be boorish, unpolished. By contrast, those who joke in a tasteful way are called ready-witted, which is a mean and a virtue.

Tact also belongs to the middle state; it is the sign of a tactful man to say and listen to such things as befit a good and well-bred man, even while jesting or joking.

Shame is not a virtue. It is more like a feeling than an aspect of character, a feeling that warns us away from disgrace. This feeling is not becoming to every age, but only to youth. Young people should be prone to feelings of shame because they live by feeling and therefore commit many errors; but shame can help to restrain them. We praise young people who are prone to this feeling, but no one would praise an older person for being fearful of disgrace, since we believe he should never be at risk of disgracing himself.

Book Five

WITH REGARD TO justice and injustice, we must (1) consider what kind of actions they are concerned with, (2) determine what sort of mean justice is, and (3) identify the extremes between which the just act is intermediate.

A state may be recognized from its contrary. If good physical condition is firmness of flesh, it follows that bad condition should be flabbiness of flesh and the wholesome should be that which causes firmness in flesh.

For the most part, if one contrary is ambiguous, the other will also be ambiguous: e.g., if "just" is so, "unjust" will be so too. Now, "justice" and "injustice" seem to be ambiguous, but their different meanings are closely related.

Let us take as a starting point, then, the various definitions of "an unjust man." Both the lawless man and the grasping, unfair man are thought to be unjust, so evidently both the law-abiding and the fair man will be just.

Since the lawless man is seen to be unjust and the law-abiding man just, evidently all lawful acts are in a sense just behavior, for the acts laid down by the legislative art are lawful, and each of these, we say, is just. The laws aim at the common advantage either of all or of the best or of those who hold power. They should produce and preserve the best life and its components for the political society. Laws bid us to be brave (e.g., not to desert our post or take to flight or throw away our arms); to be temperate (e.g., not to commit adultery or gratify our lust); and to be good-tempered (e.g., not to strike another or speak evil); and so on. Abiding by this legal form of justice, then, is complete virtue, at least in relation to our neighbors. This justice is often thought to be the greatest of virtues, and "neither evening nor morning star" is so wonderful. It is complete virtue, because he who possesses it can exercise his virtue not only in himself but also towards his neighbors. However, the best man is not he who exercises his virtue towards himself but he who exercises it towards another. Why? Because this is a difficult task.

The unjust has been divided into the unlawful and the unfair, but these terms are as different as a part differs from its whole, for all that is unfair is unlawful, but not all that is unlawful is unfair. The majority of the acts required by the law are those which are prescribed from the point of view of virtue taken as a whole: that is, the law bids us practice every virtue and forbids us to practice any vice.

Of fairness (or justice interpreted as fairness), one kind is that manifested in distributions of honor, money, and other things to be divided among those who have a share in the constitution; in these it is possible for one man to have a share either unequal or equal to that of another. Another kind is that manifested in transactions between men. Of these, some transactions are voluntary, others involuntary. The voluntary include such transactions as sale, purchase, loan for consumption, pledging, loan for use, depositing and letting; they are called voluntary because their origin is voluntary. Of the involuntary, some are clandestine (e.g., theft, adultery, poisoning, procuring, enticement of slaves, assassination, false witness) and others are violent (assault, imprisonment, murder, robbery with violence, mutilation, abuse, insult, etc.).

❦

The man who acts unjustly may receive too much of what is good; the man who is treated unjustly, too little. Unjust distribution violates proportion. To be fair, a distribution must be proportional.

❦

Just as a distribution must be proportional, so must a transaction be. It makes no difference whether a good man has defrauded a bad man or a bad man a good one, nor whether it is a good or bad man who has committed adultery. The law looks only to the distinctive character of the injury and treats the parties in the same way, whether one is in the wrong and the other is being wronged, whether one inflicted injury and the other was injured. By means of the penalty, the judge tries to restore proportion. In this case, the just is intermediate between a disproportionate gain and a disproportionate loss.

❦

The Pythagoreans defined justice, without qualification, as reciprocity. And yet, reciprocity and transactional justice do not always accord: for example, if an official has inflicted a wound, he should not be wounded in return; but if someone has wounded an official, he ought not only be wounded but also incur an additional punishment.

In any exchange—even a transaction between people as different and disproportional as a doctor and a farmer—the transaction must be proportional and thus reciprocal. To assure that all things exchanged are somehow comparable is why money was introduced as an intermediate. Money measures all things and calculates how many shoes are equal to a house or to a given amount of food.

If men did not need one another's goods, or did not need them equally, there would be either no exchange or not the same exchange. But money has become, by convention, a sort of representative of demand, and this is why it has the name "money" (*nomisma*): because it exists not by nature but by law (*nomos*), and it is in our power to change it and make it useless. It is plain that exchanges took place even before there was money, for it makes no difference whether it is five beds that are exchanged for a house or the money value of five beds.

Can a man treat himself unjustly?

The law does not expressly permit suicide, and what it does not expressly permit it forbids. He who through anger voluntarily stabs himself does this contrary to the right rule of life, and this the law does not allow; therefore, he is acting unjustly. But toward whom? Surely toward the state, not toward himself.

On the ground that he is treating the state unjustly, the state deprives of certain civil rights the man who wounds or destroys himself.

The "just" and the "unjust" always involve more than one person. No one acts unjustly without committing particular acts of injustice; but no one can commit adultery with his own wife or housebreaking on his own house or theft on his own property.

Book Six

SINCE WE HAVE previously said that one ought to choose that which is intermediate, neither excessive nor deficient, and that the intermediate is determined by the right rule, let us now discuss the nature of that rule.

In all the states of character we have mentioned, there is a mark to which a man looks, and heightens or relaxes his activity accordingly. Such a statement, though true, is by no means clear. If a man had only this knowledge, he would be none the wiser. We would not know what sort of medicines to apply to our body if someone were to say "all those which the medical art prescribes, and which agree with the practice of one who possesses the art."

We divided the virtues of the soul and said that some are virtues of character, others virtues of intellect. Now, having discussed the moral virtues of character, we will express a view with regard to the virtues of intellect.

———— ❧ ————

Moral virtue is a state of character concerned with choice, and choice is deliberate. If the choice is to be good, the reasoning must be true and the desire right. This kind of intellectual reasoning is practical.

The reasoning that is contemplative is concerned with truth and falsity, while practical reasoning is concerned with aligning truth with choice.

Our choice will not be right without practical wisdom. But it is not supreme over philosophic wisdom (i.e., over the superior part of us), any more than the art of medicine is superior to health.

———— ❧ ————

One of the ways we arrive at truth is through science, which—as we maintain in the *Analytics*—proceeds sometimes through induction and sometimes by syllogism.

———— ❧ ————

Wisdom is the most finished of the many forms of knowledge.

The wise man must not only know what follows from the first principles but also possess knowledge of the first principles. Therefore, wisdom must combine intuitive reason with scientific knowledge—knowledge of the highest objects, such as the bodies framing the heavens.

Practical wisdom, on the other hand, is concerned with things human.

———— ❦ ————

That practical wisdom is not scientific knowledge is evident; for as has been said, it is concerned with particular facts that guide what is to be done. Practical wisdom is concerned with actions.

———— ❦ ————

Practical and philosophic wisdom are both virtues, but of different parts of the soul.

It would be strange if practical wisdom, being inferior to philosophic wisdom, were to be put in authority over it, as seems to be implied by the fact that it guides and rules our actions.

———— ❦ ————

Socrates, in thinking that all the virtues are forms of practical wisdom, was wrong. But in saying they implied practical wisdom, he was right.

Book Seven

LET US NOW make a fresh beginning and point out that of the moral states to be avoided, there are three kinds: vice, lack of self-control, brutishness. The contraries of two of these are evident; one we call virtue, the other continence. To the third—brutishness—it would be most fitting to oppose superhuman virtue, a heroic and divine kind of virtue. As Homer sang of Priam, praising his son Hector:

> For he seemed not, he,
> The child of a mortal man, but as one
>   that of
> God's seed came.

If, as they say, men become gods by excess of virtue, this must be the state opposed to the brutish state; a brute has neither vice nor virtue, but neither has a god. The god's state is higher than virtue; brutishness is a different kind of state from vice.

When the Spartans admire anyone highly, they call him a "godlike man." Just as godlike men are rare, so, too, the brutish type is seldom found among men; it is found chiefly among barbarians. Some brutish qualities are produced by disease or deformity. We also call by this evil name those men who go beyond all ordinary standards by reason of vice.

We have already discussed vice. Now we must discuss lack of self-control and softness (i.e., effeminacy), contrasted with self-control and endurance (the two are neither identical with virtue or wickedness, nor of a different genus).

We may ask how a man who judges rightly can behave without self-control.

That he should behave so when he has knowledge, Socrates thought impossible, for it would be strange (so Socrates thought) if when a man had knowledge, something else could master him and drag him about like a slave. Therefore, Socrates held that there is no such thing as incontinence; that no one, having judged, acts against what he judges best; that people act so only by reason of ignorance.

But this view contradicts the observable facts. The man who behaves incontinently does not, before he gets into this state, think he ought to act so.

We can disregard the sophistic argument, which holds that folly coupled with incontinence is virtue, since a man does the opposite of what he judges, owing to incontinence. Judging what is good to be evil and something that he should not do, in consequence he will do what is good and not what is evil.

———⟊———

We must next discuss whether there is anyone who lacks self-control generally, without qualification, or if every man who lacks self-control does so in a particular sense, losing control only when confronting certain things.

Of the things that produce pleasure, some are necessary while others are worthy of choice in themselves but may lead to excess. Pleasures associated with food and with sexual intercourse (i.e., the physical pleasures) are necessary. Others are unnecessary but worthy of choice in themselves (e.g., victory, honor, wealth, and other good and pleasant things of this sort).

———⟊———

We pardon people more easily for following natural desires, since these appetites are common to all men.

———⟊———

With regard to the pleasures, pains, appetites, and aversions arising through touch and taste, it is possible to be defeated even by those which most people master, and to master those which defeat most people.

Most people fall into the intermediate degree but lean more towards the worse states.

One example of lack of self-control is impetuosity. Some men deliberate but then—owing to emotion—fail to stand by the conclusion of their deliberation. Others do not deliberate and are led by their emotions.

———— ❧ ————

Generally speaking, incontinence and vice differ in kind. Vice is unconscious of itself, incontinence is conscious. But they are similar with respect to the actions they lead to.

People who lack self-control are not criminal, but they will perform criminal acts.

———— ❧ ————

No one can have practical wisdom who lacks self-control. A man displays practical wisdom not solely by knowing but also by being able to act in the right way.

Of the many forms of lack of self-control, that of excitable people is more curable than that of those who deliberate but do not abide by their decisions. Those who lack self-control through habit are easier to cure than those in whom incontinence is innate, for it is easier to change a habit than to change one's nature. But even habit is hard to change.

Some people think that no pleasure can be a good, either in itself or incidentally, since the good and pleasure are not the same. Others think that some pleasures are good but most are bad. There is a third view: that even if all pleasures are good, the best thing in the world cannot be pleasure.

The reasons given for the view that no pleasures are ever good are: (a) every pleasure is only a means to an end; (b) a temperate man avoids pleasures; (c) a man of practical wisdom pursues what is free from pain, not what is pleasant; (d) pleasures hinder thought, the more so the more one delights in them (e.g., in sexual pleasure), and no one can think of anything else while absorbed in this; (e) there is no art of pleasure, but every good is the product of some art; (f) children and the brutes pursue pleasures.

The reasons for the view that not every pleasure is good include: (a) there are pleasures that are actually base and objects of reproach; and (b) there are harmful pleasures, for some pleasant things are unhealthy. The reason for the view that pleasure is not the best thing in the world is that pleasure is not an end but a means.

These are pretty much the arguments. It does not follow from them that pleasure is not a good, or even the chief good; it is more complicated than that. For example, neither practical wisdom nor any desirable state of being is impeded by the pleasure arising from it. Indeed, the pleasures arising from thinking and learning will make us think and learn all the more.

It is agreed that pain is bad and to be avoided. Some pain is without qualification bad; other pain is bad because it is in some respect an impediment to us. Now, the contrary of that which is to be avoided because it is bad must be good. Pleasure, then, is necessarily a good. The answer of Speusippus—that pleasure is contrary both to pain and to good, as the greater is contrary both to the lesser and to the equal—is unsuccessful, since he would not say that pleasure is essentially just a species of evil.

If certain pleasures are bad, that does not prevent the chief good from being some form of pleasure, just as the chief good may be some form of knowledge even though certain kinds of knowledge are bad. All men—thinking that living the best life is pleasant— weave pleasure into their ideal of the best life. Those who say that the victim on the rack or the man who falls into great misfortunes is living the best life (so long as he is good) are talking nonsense. Because we need good fortune as well as other things, some people believe good fortune to be the same thing as the best life. But it is not, since even good fortune in excess is an impediment, and—because it will cost us the best life—should no longer be called good fortune.

Even the fact that both brutes and men pursue pleasure is an indication of its somehow being the chief good. Although they do not all pursue the *same* pleasure, yet all pursue pleasure. It may be that they actually pursue not the pleasure they think they are pursuing (let alone that which they say they pursue), but some other, similar pleasure; for all beings have by nature something divine in them. The physical pleasures have appropriated the name of pleasure both because we most often steer our course toward them and because all men share in them. Just because they are the most familiar, men think there are no others.

If pleasure is neither an evil nor a good, it follows that pain is not either. Why then avoid it? Because the life of the good man will be more pleasant than that of anyone else, since his activities will afford more pleasure.

With regard to the physical pleasures, those who say that some pleasures are very much to be chosen (the noble pleasures, but not the physical pleasures) must consider why, then, the contrary pains, such as hunger, are bad. And we must keep in mind that all men enjoy, in some way or other, special foods, choice wines, and sexual intercourse. (Granted, not all men enjoy these as they ought.)

We should also explore why some deem the physical pleasures the more worthy of choice.

Firstly, it is because these expel pain; and men who experience excesses of pain seek relief in excessive physical pleasure—and curative agencies produce intense feeling. Secondly, because of their very intensity, certain physical pleasures are pursued by those incapable of other pleasures.

Because our nature is not simple, there is no one thing that is always pleasant. If one element of our nature leads us somewhere, another element dissents. Consequently, pleasure is found more in rest than in movement.

Book Eight

AFTER WHAT WE have said, a discussion of friendship follows naturally, since it is a virtue, or implies virtue, and is besides most necessary to our life. Without friends no one would choose to live, though he had all other goods. Even rich men and those in high office are thought to need friends most of all. What is the use of prosperity without the opportunity of sharing it, which is done in its most laudable form with friends? How can prosperity (which, the greater it is, is the more exposed to risk) be preserved without friends? In poverty and other misfortunes, men think friends their only refuge.

Friendship helps keep the young from error, aids older people by ministering to their needs and stimulates those in the prime of life to noble actions ("two going together"). A man with friends is better able to think and to act.

By nature, it seems, parents feel friendship for offspring and offspring for their parents, not only among men but also among birds and among most animals. It is felt mutually by members of the same race, and especially by men. Friendship seems to hold states together; indeed, lawgivers care more for it than for justice. Unanimity appears to be something like friendship, and at this legislators aim at most of all, regarding factions as their worst enemies. When men are true friends, they have no need of justice; but even when they are just, they require friendship, too. The truest form of justice is thought to be a quality of friendly feeling.

Friendship is not only necessary; it is noble. And so, believing good men and friends to be one and the same, we praise those who love their friends and honor those who have many friends.

And yet, some things about friendship are matters of debate.

Empedocles and others define it as a kind of likeness, insisting that similar people are more apt to become friends (hence the sayings "Birds of a feather flock together," "like to like," etc.). Others disagree, saying, "Two of a trade never agree." Euripides wrote that "parched earth loves the rain, and stately heaven when filled with rain loves to fall to earth." Heraclitus maintained "it is what opposes that helps," "from different tones comes the fairest tune," and "all things are produced through strife." So let us examine whether friendship can arise between any two people, whether people cannot be friends if they are wicked, and whether there is more than one species of friendship.

———— ❧ ————

The kinds of friendship may best be understood if we first come to know the object of love. Not everything seems to be loved, only the lovable: namely, the good, pleasant, or useful.

The good and the useful are lovable as ends. But it is fair to ask: do men love the good, or what is good for them? These sometimes clash. So, too, with regard to the pleasant. Now, it is thought that each man loves what is good for himself, that this good is without qualification lovable, and what is good for each man is lovable for him. That men love not what is good for them but what *seems* good makes no difference; we shall have to settle on calling it "that which seems lovable."

Of a friend we say we ought to wish what is good for his sake. When the wish is reciprocal, it is friendship. Or must we add "when it is recognized," since many people feel goodwill for those whom they have never seen but judge to be good or useful; and one of these strangers might return the feeling. These people seem to bear goodwill to each other, but how could we call them friends when they do not know their mutual feelings? To be friends, then, both must be mutually recognized as bearing goodwill and wishing well to the other.

———— ❧ ————

There are three kinds of friendship, equal in number to the things that are lovable.

Those who love each other for their utility do not love each other for themselves but because of some good they gain from each other. So, too, with those who love for the sake of pleasure; it is not for their character that men love entertaining people, but because they find them enjoyable. These friendships, being only incidental, are easily dissolved should one party be no longer pleasant or useful, and the other cease to love him.

This kind of friendship is seen chiefly between old people (for at that age people pursue not the pleasant but the useful). They seldom live with each other; sometimes they fail to find each other pleasant. Among such friendships people also class that of a host and guest.

For the most part, the friendship of young people aims at pleasure. They live under the guidance of emotion, and pursue above all what is pleasant to themselves and what is immediately before them. With increasing age, their pleasures change. This is why the young become friends quickly and as quickly cease to be so. Their friendship varies with the object found pleasant, and such pleasure alters swiftly. Young people are also amorous. Because the greater part of their friendship depends on "being in love" and aims at pleasure, their friendships often change within a single day. But these people *do* wish to spend their days, indeed their lives, together, for it is thus they hope to attain the purpose of their friendship.

Perfect friendship is the friendship of men who are good and alike in virtue. Those who wish their friends well for their sake are most truly friends; their friendship lasts as long as they are good—and goodness endures. The good are both good without qualification and useful to each other. Plus, both men find the other's activities pleasurable. As might be expected, such a friendship is permanent, since it represents all the qualities that friends should have. Love and friendship, therefore, are found most often and in their best form between men with these qualities.

But such men are rare. Furthermore, such a friendship requires time and familiarity. As the proverb says, men cannot know each other till they have "eaten salt together"; nor can they admit each other to friendship until both have found the other to be lovable and trustworthy.

A wish for friendship may arise quickly, but friendship does not.

In a perfect friendship, each gets from each in all respects what he gives, which is what ought to happen between friends. Also among men of the inferior sort, friendships are most permanent when the friends receive the same thing from each other. This does not happen between lover and beloved, for they do not take pleasure in the same thing; the one delights in seeing his beloved, the other in receiving attentions from his lover. When the bloom of youth passes, the friendship sometimes passes, too, the one finding no pleasure in the sight of the other, the other receiving no attentions from the first. On the other hand, many lovers are constant, if familiarity has led them to love each other's characters, and those characters are similar. But those who exchange utility rather than pleasure are both less truly friends and less constant. Those who are friends for the sake of utility part when the advantage is at an end; they befriended profit, not each other.

For the sake of pleasure or utility, then, even bad men may be friends of each other, or good men of bad; one who is neither good nor bad may be a friend to any sort of person. But only good men can be friends for friendship's sake; bad men do not delight in each other unless they derive some advantage from the relationship.

Only the friendship of the good is proof against slander. It is among good men that trust and the feeling that "he would never wrong me" are found. In the other kinds of friendship, there is nothing to prevent distrust from arising. For example, men apply the name of "friends" even to those whose motive is utility (e.g., allied states), and to those who love each other for the sake of pleasure, the case with children said to be "friends." Acknowledging that there are several kinds of friendship, we may call such states and people friends so long as we remember that in the proper sense, the friendship of good men ranks first.

Just as with regard to the virtues—some men being called good with respect to the state of their character, others with respect to an activity—so, too, in the case of friendship.

Distance does not break off a friendship absolutely, only the activity of it. But if the absence is lasting, it seems to make men forget their friendship; hence the saying "out of sight, out of mind." Neither old people nor sour people make friends easily. There is little that is pleasant in them, and nobody can spend his days with one whose company is painful or unpleasant, since nature seems above all to avoid the painful and to aim at the pleasant. Those, however, who approve of each other but do not live together, seem to be well disposed rather than actual friends; there is nothing so characteristic of friends as living together. Even those who live the best life desire to spend their days together, for solitude suits such people least of all. But people cannot live together as companion friends if they are not pleasant and do not enjoy the same things.

─────❧─────

There is another kind of friendship: namely, that which involves an inequality between the parties, e.g., that of father to son and in general of elder to younger; that of man to wife; and in general that of ruler to subject. The friendship between parents and children is not the same as between rulers and subjects. Neither is that of father to son the same as that of son to father, nor is that of husband to wife the same as that of wife to husband. The virtue and the function of each is different, and the reasons for which they love; the love and the friendship are therefore different, too. Each party, then, neither gets the same from the other, nor ought to seek it. When children render to parents what they ought to render to those who brought them into the world, and parents render what they should to their children, the friendship of such persons will be abiding and excellent. In all friendships implying inequality, the love, too, should be proportional: That is, the virtuous should be loved more than he whom he loves, and so should the more useful. When the love is in proportion to the merits of the parties, then there arises that equality which is held to be characteristic of friendship.

Equality does not seem to take the same form in acts of justice and in friendship. In acts of justice, what is equal in the primary sense is that which is in proportion to merit; quantitative equality is secondary. But in friendship, quantitative equality is primary and proportion-to-merit secondary. This becomes clear if the parties differ greatly in virtue, wealth, or anything else. In that case, they are no longer friends and do not even expect to be so. This is most manifest in the case of the gods, for they surpass us decisively in all good things. But it is also apparent in the case of kings, for with them, too, men who are much their inferiors do not expect to be their friends. Nor do men of no account expect to be friends with the best or wisest men. In such cases, it is impossible to define up to what exact point friends can remain friends. Much can be taken away and friendship remain, but when one party is removed to a great distance, as God is, the possibility of friendship ceases. This is the origin of the question whether friends truly wish for their friends the greatest good (e.g., to be gods), since in that case their friends will no longer be friends to them and, therefore, will not be good for them (as we have said, having friends is good).

It is for himself most of all that every man wishes what is good.

Most people wish to be loved rather than to love; this is why they hunger for flattery. The flatterer—a friend in an inferior position (or behaving as such)—pretends to love more than he is loved. Being loved seems akin to being honored, and this is what most people aim at. But it is not for its own sake that people want to be honored; they usually want something else.

On the other hand, people do delight in being loved for its own sake. Since friendship depends more on loving than honor, and it is those who love their friends who are praised, loving seems to be the characteristic virtue of friends. It is only those in whom this virtue is found in due measure who are lasting friends. Only their friendship endures.

It is friendship for utility's sake that most easily exists between contraries, e.g., between poor and rich, between the ignorant and learned; for what a man lacks he aims at—and receives something else in return. Under this head, we might class the lover and beloved one of whom is beautiful, the other ugly. These lovers seem ridiculous to others.

The proverb "What friends have is common property" expresses the truth, since friendship depends on community. Brothers and comrades hold all things in common, but friends also share specific things—

some more things, others fewer; for among friendships some are more, and others less, truly friendships.

Claims of justice differ. The duties of parents to children and those of brothers to each other are not the same; nor are those of comrades and those of fellow-citizens. And so it is with the different kinds of friendship. It is a more terrible thing to defraud a comrade than a fellow citizen, worse not to help a brother than a stranger, and more terrible to wound a father than anyone else. The demands of justice seem to increase with the intensity of the friendship.

Forms of friendship, like other forms of community, are part of a larger political community.

———— ❦ ————

There are three kinds of constitution, and an equal number of deviations (in truth, perversions of them). The constitutions are monarchy, aristocracy, and that which is based on a property qualification (this it seems appropriate to call timocratic). The best of these is monarchy, the worst timocracy.

The perversion of monarchy is tyranny. Both take the form of one-man rule, but there is the greatest difference between them: the tyrant looks solely to his own advantage, the good king to that of his subjects. A man is not a king unless he is sufficient to himself and excels his subjects in all good things. Such a man needs nothing further; therefore, he looks not to his own interests but to those of his subjects. A king who is not like that would be a king in name only. Tyranny is the very opposite of this; the tyrant pursues his own good. The worst form of government is thus a perversion of the best. Monarchy may pass over into tyranny when the bad king becomes a tyrant.

Just so, aristocracy may pass over into oligarchy. In this case, bad rulers distribute the city's goods contrary to equity, keeping all or most of the choicest things to themselves and, greedy for wealth, repeatedly granting office to the same people—people willing to buy privilege.

Timocracy may pass over into democracy, since all who meet the property qualification count as equals. Democracy is the least bad of the three perversions.

One may find echoes of these constitutions even within households. The association of a father with his sons resembles monarchy, since the father cares for his children. This is why Homer calls Zeus "Father." The ideal monarchy is a paternal rule, but among the Persians the rule of the father is tyrannical; they use their sons as slaves. Tyrannical, too, is the rule of a master over slaves, for it is the master's advantage that matters in all situations.

The association of man and wife seems to be aristocratic. The man rules in accordance with his position, and in those areas in which a man should rule; but the matters that befit a woman he hands over to her. If the man rules in everything, the relation passes over into oligarchy, for in doing so he is not acting in accordance with their respective positions. Sometimes women rule, because they are heiresses. Their rule is not by virtue of excellence, but due to wealth and power, as in oligarchies.

The association of brothers is like timocracy; they are equal, except insofar as they differ in age. If their ages differ by much, the friendship is no longer of the fraternal type. Democracy is found chiefly in dwellings with no master (for here everyone is equal), but also in those in which the ruler is weak and everyone has license to do as he pleases.

In the perverted constitutional forms, justice hardly exists and friendship is rare (it exists least in the worst form). In tyranny there is little or no friendship. Although in tyrannies justice and friendship hardly exist, in democracies they exist more fully; for where the citizens are equal, they have much in common.

Book Nine

A FURTHER PROBLEM IS defined by such questions as whether one should, in all things, give priority to one's father and obey him; whether when ill one should trust a doctor; whether one should render a service first to a friend or to a good man; and whether to show gratitude to a benefactor or oblige a friend, if one cannot do both.

Because they involve all sorts of variations, such questions are hard to decide with precision. That we should not give the preference in all things to the same person is plain enough. We must, for the most part, return benefits rather than oblige friends, as we must pay back a loan to a creditor rather than make one to a friend. But perhaps even this is not always true. For example, should a man who has been ransomed out of the hands of brigands ransom his ransomer in return—whoever he may be—or should he ransom his father? It would seem that he should ransom his father in preference even to himself.

As we have said, generally the debt should be paid, but sometimes it is not fair to return the equivalent of what one has received. For example, you should not lend an additional sum to a man who earlier lent to yourself if he lent to a good man (you) expecting to recover his loan, while you have no hope of recovering from him, whom you believe to be bad. If these are the facts, his demand is not fair.

That we should not make the same return to everyone nor give a father the preference in all matters (as one does not sacrifice everything to Zeus) is plain enough. Since we ought to render different things to parents, brothers, comrades, and benefactors, we ought to render to each class what is appropriate and becoming. To all older persons one should give honor appropriate to their age by rising to receive them, finding seats for them, and so on; while to comrades and brothers one should allow freedom of speech and common use of all things. To kinsmen, fellow tribesmen, fellow citizens, and every other class, one should try to assign what is appropriate, and to compare the claims of each class with respect to their nearness of relation, virtue, or usefulness. The comparison is easier when the persons belong to the same class, more laborious when they are different. Yet we must not on that account shrink from the task but, rather, decide the question as best we can.

———— ❦ ————

Another question that arises is whether friendships should or should not be broken off when the other party does not remain the same. There is nothing strange in breaking off a friendship based on utility or pleasure when our friends no longer demonstrate these attributes. It was those attributes that brought us together as friends; and when these have failed, it is reasonable to love no longer. But one might complain of another if, when he loved us for our usefulness or pleasantness, he pretended to love us for our character. As we said at the outset, most differences between friends arise when they are not friends in the spirit in which they believed they were. So when a man has deceived himself and has thought he was being loved for his character when, in fact, the other person was doing nothing of the kind, he must blame himself. When he has been deceived by the other's pretences, it is fair for him to complain about his deceiver. He will complain with more justice than one does against people who counterfeit currency, for the wrongdoing is concerned with something more valuable.

But if one accepts another man as good, and he proves himself to be bad, must one still love him? Surely it is impossible, since not everything can be loved, but only what is good. What is evil neither can nor should be loved. It is not one's duty to be a lover of evil, or to become like the bad. Must the friendship, then, be broken off forthwith—or only when one's friend is incurable in his wickedness? If he is capable of being reformed, one should rather come to the assistance of his character or property, inasmuch as this is better and more characteristic of friendship. But a man who breaks off such a friendship would seem to be doing nothing strange; it was not a man of this sort whom he befriended. When his friend has changed, and he is unable to save him, he quite rightly gives him up.

But if one friend remained the same while the other became better, far outstripping him in virtue, should the latter treat the former as a friend? Surely he cannot. If one friend remained a child in intellect while the other became a fully developed man, how can they now be friends when they neither approve of the same things nor delight in and are pained by the same things?

———— ❧ ————

Existence is good to the virtuous man, and each man wishes the good for himself, but no one chooses to possess the whole world if he has first to become someone else. Such a man wishes to live with himself. He does so with pleasure, since the memories of his past acts are delightful; and his hopes for the future are good and, therefore, pleasant; his mind is well stored with subjects of contemplation. He has, so to speak, nothing to repent of.

Therefore, since each of these characteristics belongs to the good man in relation to himself, and he is related to his friend as to himself (for his friend is another self), it is said that friendship, too, is one of these attributes and that he who shares these attributes is his friend.

Bad men, by contrast, are weighed down with repentance. Because there is nothing in him to love, the bad man does not seem to be amicably disposed even to himself. If to be thus is the height of wretchedness, we should strain every nerve to avoid wickedness and endeavor to be good, for only in this way can one be either friendly to oneself or a friend to another.

Benefactors are thought to love those they have benefited, even more than those who have been well treated love their benefactors. (This is often discussed as though it were paradoxical.) Most people think it is because the beneficiaries are in the position of debtors and the benefactors of creditors. In the case of loans, debtors wish that their creditors had ceased to exist, while creditors actually guard the safety of their debtors. In a similar way, it is thought that benefactors wish the objects of their action to keep on living, since they will then repay their debts of gratitude. That the beneficiaries do not return the compliment Epicharmus explains by saying that this is because they "look at things on their bad side." In fact, it is quite like human nature; most people are forgetful, more anxious to be well treated than to treat others well.

Yet the cause of this phenomenon would seem to be more deeply rooted in the nature of things. The case of those who have lent money is not even analogous. Lenders have no friendly feeling toward their debtors, only a wish that they be kept safe until the debt is paid. By contrast, those who have done a service to others feel friendship and love for those they have served even if these are not of any use to them and never will be. This is what happens with craftsmen too; every man loves his own handiwork. Just so, benefactors love their "handiwork." The reason for this is that existence is to all men a thing to be chosen and loved; we exist by virtue of activity (i.e., by living and acting), and our handiwork moves us to love existence. This is rooted in the nature of things.

The benefactor delights in the object of his action, which strikes him as noble. What is pleasant is the activity of the present, the hope of the future, and the memory of the past. But most pleasant—and, therefore, most lovable—is that which depends on activity.

Men love more what they have won by labor. Those who have earned their money value it more than those who have inherited wealth. To be well treated seems to involve no labor, while to treat others well is a laborious task. These are also the reasons why mothers are fonder of their children than are fathers: bringing a child into the world costs a woman more pains (and they know better that the child is their own).

The question is also debated whether a man should love himself—or someone else—most. People criticize those who love themselves most, and call them self-lovers, using this as an epithet of disgrace. A bad man seems to do everything for his own sake (the more so, the more wicked he is), and so men reproach him. The good man acts for honor's sake—sacrificing his own interest for his friend—and the more so the better he is.

Not surprisingly, the facts clash with these arguments. If one is to love others, is one not to love oneself? If the proverbs agree (e.g., "a single soul," "What friends have is common property," "Friendship is equality," "Charity begins at home"), does this not apply to a man's relation to himself? He is his own best friend and ought to love himself best. Which of the two views should we follow, for both are plausible? Perhaps we ought to separate such arguments from each other and determine how far, and in what respects, each view is right. If we grasp the sense in which each school uses the phrase "lover of self," the truth may surface.

Those who use the term as one of reproach ascribe self-love to people who assign to themselves the greater share of wealth, honors, and physical pleasures. These are what most people desire and busy themselves with as though they were the best of all things; it's also the reason why they become objects of competition. Those who covet these things gratify their appetites and in general their feelings and the irrational element of the soul; most men are of this nature. It is just that men who are lovers of self in this way are reproached for being so.

If, on the other hand, a man was always anxious that he himself, above all things, should act justly, temperately, or in accordance with any other of the virtues, and in general was always trying to steer the honorable course, no one would call such a man a lover of self or blame him. All would praise him.

But just such a man would seem—more than the other—to be a true lover of self. At all events, he assigns to himself the things that are noblest and best, and lives according to the most rational principle. If all were to strive towards what is noble and strain every nerve to do the noblest deeds, everything would be as it should be for the commonweal, and everyone would secure for himself the goods that are greatest, since virtue is the greatest of goods.

Therefore, the good man *should* be a lover of self, for he will profit by doing noble acts and benefiting his fellows; but the wicked man should not, since he will hurt both himself and his neighbors, following as he does evil passions. What the wicked man does clashes with what he ought to do, but what the good man ought to do he does. The good man does many acts for the sake of his friends and his country, and if necessary dies for them. He will throw away both wealth and honors and, in general, the goods that are objects of competition, in the process gaining nobility for himself. He would prefer a short period of intense pleasure to a long one of mild enjoyment, a twelve-month of noble life to many years of humdrum existence, one great and noble action to many trivial ones. Those who die for others doubtless attain this result; it is, therefore, a great prize that they choose for themselves. They will also throw away wealth on condition that their friends gain more; for while a man's friend gains wealth, he himself achieves nobility, thereby assigning the greater good to himself. The same is true of honor and office: all these things he will sacrifice to his friend, as this is noble and laudable for himself. Rightly, then, is he thought to be good, since he chooses nobility over all else. But he may even abandon action for the sake of his friend, as it may be more noble to become the cause of his friend's acting than to act himself.

In all the actions men are praised for, the good man is seen to assign to himself the greater share in what is noble. In this sense a man should be a lover of self—but in the sense evidenced by the majority, he ought not.

———— ❧ ————

It is also debated whether they who live the best life require friends or not. They have the things that are good and, being self-sufficient, nothing beyond that. But it seems strange, when one assigns all good things to such men, not to assign them friends, who are thought the greatest of external goods. And if it is more characteristic of a friend to do well by another than to be well done by, the good man will need people to do well by. It is strange, too, to condemn him who lives the best life to a solitary existence. No one would choose the whole world on condition of being alone, since man is a political creature and one whose nature is to live with others.

What, then, is it that the first school means, and in what respect is it right? Is it that most identify friends with useful people? Of such friends, he who lives the best life will have no need, since he already has the things that are good. Nor will he need those whom one befriends because of their pleasantness (or he will need them only to a small extent). Because he does not need such friends, he is thought to need no friends at all.

But that is surely untrue. As we said at the outset, (1) if the best life lies in living and being active, and the good man's activity is virtuous and pleasant in itself; (2) if a thing's being one's own helps to make it pleasant; (3) if we can contemplate our neighbors better than ourselves and their actions better than our own; and (4) if the actions of virtuous men who are their friends are pleasant to good men, then the man who lives the best life will need friends of this sort, since his purpose is to contemplate worthy actions— his own actions as well as those of a good man who is his friend.

If we look deeper into the nature of things, a virtuous friend seems to be naturally desirable for a virtuous man, for that which is desirable for him he must have, or he will be deficient in this respect. The man who is to live the best life requires virtuous friends.

Book Ten

AFTER THESE MATTERS, we ought to return to a discussion of pleasure.

Eudoxus thought pleasure was the greatest good because he saw all things, both rational and irrational, as aiming at it; and because in all things, that which is the object of choice is what is excellent, and that which is most the object of choice is the greatest good. The fact that all things move toward the same object indicates that this is for all things the chief good, since each thing, he argued, finds its own good, as it finds its own nourishment. (Eudoxus' arguments were credited more for the excellence of his character than for their own sake. Because he was held to be remarkably self-controlled, men trusted that he was no slave of pleasure and, therefore, spoke the truth—despite the facts.)

Eudoxus believed that the same conclusion followed from a study of pain, the contrary of pleasure. Because pain is an object of aversion to all things, its opposite must similarly be an object of choice. Again, that is most an object of choice which we choose not because of—or for the sake of—something else, and pleasure is admittedly of this nature. That no one asks to what end he is pleased implies that pleasure is in itself an object of choice. Further, Eudoxus argued that 1) pleasure when added to any good, e.g., to just or temperate action, makes it more worthy of choice, and 2) it is only by itself that the good can be increased.

This argument seems to show pleasure to be *one* of the goods, and no more a good than any other; also that every good is more worthy of choice when accompanied by another good than when taken alone. It is by an argument of this kind that Plato proves that pleasure is not the greatest good. He argues that the pleasant life is more desirable with wisdom than without, and that if the mixture is better, pleasure is not the good, for the good cannot become more desirable by the addition of anything to it. It is clear that nothing can be the good if it is made more desirable by the addition of any of the things that are good in themselves. What, then, is there that satisfies this criterion, something we can participate in?

On the other hand, to argue that what we all aim for is *not* necessarily good does seem to be talking nonsense.

In reply to those who mention the disgraceful pleasures, one may say that these are unpleasant. Just as we do not reason that things sick people find to be wholesome, sweet, or bitter are also pleasant to the healthy, and just as we do not ascribe whiteness to things that seem white to those suffering from a disease of the eye: if things are pleasant to people of vicious constitution, we must not suppose that they are also pleasant to others. Put another way: the pleasures are desirable, but not wealth amassed by betrayal. Likewise, health is to be desired but not at the cost of eating anything and everything. Or perhaps pleasures differ in kind. Those derived from noble sources are different from those derived from base sources, and one cannot experience the pleasure of the just man without being just, nor that of the musical man without being musical, and so on.

There are many things we should be keen on even if they brought no pleasure (e.g., seeing, remembering, knowing, possessing the virtues). If pleasures necessarily accompany these, that makes no difference; we should choose these even if no pleasure resulted. It seems to be clear, then, that neither is pleasure the good nor are all pleasures desirable, and that some pleasures—differing from the others in kind or in their sources—are desirable in themselves.

———— ❧ ————

How is it that no one is continuously pleased? Is it that we grow weary? Certainly all human beings are incapable of continuous activity; therefore, because it accompanies activity, pleasure is not continuous. For the same reason, some things delight us when they are new, but later less. At first the mind is in a state of active stimulation, as people are with respect to their vision when they look hard at a thing. Afterward our activity changes, grows relaxed; for this reason the pleasure also is dulled.

One might think that all men desire pleasure because they all aim at life. Life is an activity, and each man is active about those things and with those faculties which he loves most. The musician is active with his hearing in relation to tunes, the student with his mind in relation to theoretical questions, etc. Pleasure completes the activities and, therefore, the life they desire. It is with good reason, then, that they aim at pleasure, since for everyone it completes life, which is desirable. But whether we choose life for the sake of pleasure or pleasure for the sake of life is a question we may dismiss for the present.

———— ❧ ————

Activities of thought differ from those of the senses, and both differ among themselves; so do the pleasures that complete them. Pleasures differ in kind.

An activity is intensified by its proper pleasure. Those who engage in geometry with pleasure grasp the various propositions more readily. Similarly, those who are fond of music or of building, etc., make faster progress in music or architecture, thanks to their enjoyment. The pleasures intensify the activities, and what intensifies a thing is proper to it.

This will be even more apparent from the fact that activities are hindered by pleasures arising from other sources. People who are fond of playing the flute are incapable of attending to arguments if they overhear someone else playing the flute, since they enjoy flute playing more than the activity at hand. The pleasure connected with flute playing disrupts the activity of argument. This also happens when one is active about two things at once: the more pleasant activity drives out the other; and if it is much more pleasant, does so all the more. This is why when we enjoy anything very much, we do not throw ourselves into anything else. (Alien pleasures have been said to do much the same as pain; they destroy the activity, if only to a different degree.)

Since activities differ in virtue or vice, some are worthy to be chosen, others to be avoided; it is the same for the associated pleasure. The pleasure proper to a worthy activity is good and the pleasure associated with an unworthy activity bad, just as the appetites for noble objects are laudable and those for base objects deserving of censure.

Each animal is thought to have a proper pleasure: namely, that which corresponds to its activity. As Heraclitus says, "Asses would prefer sweepings to gold." The pleasures of creatures different in kind, differ in kind. It is plausible to suppose that those of a single species do not differ, but they do vary and to no small extent—at least, in the case of men. The same things delight some people and are odious to others. Those so-called pleasures that are admittedly disgraceful should not be described as pleasures, except to a perverted taste. Of those thought to be good, what kinds of pleasure may be called proper to man? Is it not plain from the corresponding activities? If he who lives the best life pursues one or more activities, the pleasures that perfect these must be proper to man.

Now that we have spoken of the virtues, the forms of friendship, and the varieties of pleasure, it remains to outline the nature of the best life, since this is what we understand the end of human nature to be. Our discussion will be the more concise if we first sum up what we have already said.

We stated that the best life is not a disposition; for if it were, it might belong to someone who slept through his entire life, living the life of a vegetable; or, again, to someone suffering the greatest misfortunes. If these so-called lives are unacceptable, we must rather class the best life as an activity. And if some activities are necessary and desirable for the sake of something else, while others are so in themselves, evidently the best life must be placed among those desirable in themselves, since the best life—lacking nothing—is self-sufficient.

Those activities are desirable in themselves from which nothing more is sought beyond the activity. Virtuous actions fall into this category.

Pleasant amusements are sometimes thought to be of this nature. Do we not choose them for themselves (although we are often injured rather than benefited by them, since they lead us to neglect our bodies and our property)? Most of the people deemed to be living the best life take refuge in such pastimes; despots spend their leisure in them.

But perhaps such people prove nothing. Virtue and reason, from which good activities flow, do not depend on absolute power. If these people, who have never tasted pure and generous pleasure, take refuge in the bodily pleasures, should they for that reason be thought more desirable? Boys, too, think the things that are valued among themselves are the best. It is to be expected, then, that just as different things seem valuable to boys and to men, bad men and good men should esteem different things. As we have often maintained, those things are both valuable and pleasant which are such to the good man.

The best life, therefore, does not lie in amusement. It would, indeed, be strange if the end were amusement, and one must take trouble and suffer hardship all one's life in order to amuse oneself. To toil for the sake of amusement seems silly, childish. But to amuse oneself in order that one may exert oneself, as Anacharsis puts it, seems right. Amusement is a form of relaxation, and we need relaxation because we cannot work continuously. Relaxation, then, is not an end; it is taken for the sake of activity.

———— ❧ ————

If the best life is activity in accordance with virtue, it is reasonable that it should be in accordance with the highest virtue. We have already identified this activity as contemplation.

We can contemplate truth more continuously than we can do anything else. The best life has pleasure mingled with it, and the activity of philosophic wisdom is admittedly the most pleasant of virtuous activities. Self-sufficiency is another feature of contemplative activity. A philosopher as well as a just man, or one possessing any other virtue, requires life's necessities. But even when sufficiently equipped with things of that sort, the just man still needs people toward whom and with whom he can act justly. The temperate man, the brave man, and all of the others are in the same situation.

The philosopher, even when by himself, can contemplate truth; his deliberations may be better if he has fellow workers, but still he is the most self-sufficient. The philosopher's activity alone would seem to be loved for its own sake: nothing arises from it apart from the contemplating, while from practical activities we gain more or less apart from the action. The best life is also thought to depend on leisure, for we busy ourselves that we may have leisure, just as we make war that we may live in peace. The activity of the practical virtues is exhibited in political or military affairs, but these actions cannot provide leisure.

Even if, among virtuous actions, political and military actions are distinguished by nobility and greatness, these are deficient in leisure; neither are they engaged in for their own sake. By contrast, the activity of reason, which is contemplative, is pursued for its own sake and meets all the criteria defining the best life.

Such a life might seem too high for man. It partakes of the divine. But we must not follow those who advise us, being men, to think only of human things—and being mortal, to dwell solely on mortal things. We must, so far as we can, make ourselves immortal and strain every nerve to live in accordance with the best in us. That which is proper to each thing is by nature best and most pleasant for each thing. For man, the life according to reason is best and most pleasant, since reason more than anything else is man's signature faculty. Therefore, a life governed by reason is also the most fulfilling.

A life lived in accordance with the other kind of virtue is the best life; it also fits our human estate. Just and brave acts, and other virtuous acts, we perform in relation to each other, observing our respective duties with regard to contracts and services and all manner of actions, and with regard to passions. Practical wisdom, too, is linked to virtue of character, since the principles of practical wisdom accord with the moral virtues and rightness in morals accords with practical wisdom. The moral virtues belong to our composite nature, and the virtues of our composite nature are human. Human, too, are the mundane life and the best life. But the excellence of the reason is a thing apart.

That the perfect, best life is a contemplative activity is apparent from the following. We assume the gods to be above all other beings blessed and living the best life; but what sort of actions must we assign to them? Acts of justice? Will not the gods seem absurd if they make contracts, return deposits, and so on? We might expect the gods to perform charitable acts, but to whom will they give? It would be strange to learn that they really have money or anything of the kind. And what would their temperate acts be? Is not such praise tasteless, since they have no bad appetites? If we were to run through them all, the spheres of action would be found trivial, unworthy of gods. Still, everyone supposes that the gods exist and, therefore, that they are active; we cannot suppose them to sleep like Endymion. Now, if you take action away from a living being—and still more, production—what is left but contemplation? Therefore the activity of God, which surpasses all others in blessedness, must be contemplative. And of human activities, that which is most contemplative must lead to the best life.

This is indicated, too, by the fact that none of the other animals live the best life, since they in no way share in contemplation. The best life extends just so far as contemplation does, and those to whom contemplation more fully belongs are living the best life more truly—not as a mere concomitant but in virtue of the contemplation, for this is precious in itself. The best life, therefore, must be some form of contemplation.

Being a man, one requires external prosperity. Our nature is not self-sufficient for the purpose of contemplation. Our body must be given food and other attention. Still, we must not think that the man who is to live the best life will require many things or great things. Self-sufficiency and action do not involve excess, and we can do noble acts without ruling earth and sea. Even with moderate advantages, one can act virtuously.

Any active man who acts in accordance with virtue will live the best life. Perhaps Solon was sketching such a man when he described him as moderately furnished with externals but living temperately. Having but modest possessions, one can still do what one ought. Anaxagoras also described the man who lives the best life as being neither rich nor a despot.

The opinions of the wise, then, seem to harmonize with our arguments, but while their opinions carry some weight, in practical matters the truth is discerned from the facts of life. They are what count. We must, therefore, recall what we have already said; test it against the facts of life; and if it harmonizes with the facts, accept it. But if it clashes with the facts, we must suppose it to be mere theory.

If arguments were in themselves enough to make men good, they would, as Theognis says, have won very great rewards. As things are, they seem to have power to encourage and stimulate the generous-minded, gently born among our youth. But they are unable to encourage the many to nobility and goodness. These do not by nature obey the sense of shame, but only fear; they do not abstain from bad acts because of those acts' baseness but only through fear of punishment. Living by passion, they pursue their own pleasures and the means to them, avoid the opposite pains, and—since they have never tasted it—have no conception of what is noble and truly pleasant. What argument would remake such people? It is hard, if not impossible, to remove by argument the traits that have long since been incorporated in the character; perhaps we must be content if, when all the influences by which we are thought to become good are present, we get some tincture of virtue.

Some think that we are made good by nature, others by habituation, others by teaching. Argument and teaching, we suspect, are not powerful with all men. He who lives as passion directs will hear no argument that dissuades him, nor understand it if he does. How can we persuade one in such a state to change his ways? In general, passion seems to yield not to argument but to force.

To live temperately is not pleasant to most people, especially when they are young. For this reason, their nurture and occupations should be fixed by law (the rules will not be painful once they become customary). But it is surely not enough that the young should receive the right nurture and attention. They must, even when they have grown up, practice and be habituated to them. We need laws for the whole of life, since most people obey necessity rather than argument, and punishments rather than a sense of what is noble.

In Sparta alone, or almost alone, the legislator seems to have paid attention to questions of nurture and day-to-day life. In most other states such matters have been neglected, and each man lives as he pleases, Cyclops-fashion, "to his own wife and children dealing law." It is best that there should be a public care for such matters. But if they are neglected by the community, it would seem right for each man to guide his children and friends towards virtue, and that men should have the power, or at least the will, to do this.

A private man can do this better if he makes himself capable of legislating, for public control is achieved by laws, and good control by good laws. Whether these are written or unwritten seems to make no difference. Further, private education has an advantage over public, just as private medical treatment surpasses public care. Although, in general, rest and abstinence from food are good for a man with a fever, for a particular man they may not be; and a boxer presumably does not prescribe the same style of fighting to all his pupils. It would seem, then, that the details are worked out with more precision if the control is private.

In the larger community, our predecessors have left the subject of legislation to us unexamined. Perhaps it is best that we should study it ourselves, and in general study the question of the constitution in order to complete—to the best of our ability—our philosophy of human nature.

Index

A

action
  best life and 22, 24
  character and 39
  compulsion and 35, 38
  friendship and 101
  from ignorance 35–38, 72
  good 30–31
  mixed 35–36
  of benefactors 97–98
  political 20
  practical wisdom 21, 68–69, 74–76, 114
  right 9, 29, 58
  self-sufficiency and 115
  the gods and 114–115
  the mean and 11, 32
  virtuous 106
  voluntary and involuntary 35–38, 46, 63
adultery 2, 11, 32, 62–66
amusement 59, 112
Analytics 68
appetite 12, 31, 36–37
  belly-gods 45–46
  incontinent man and 37
appropriately magnificent man. *See* man
appropriately proud man. *See* man
appropriate pride 52–53, 56
arête 1–2
aristocracy. *See* constitution, kinds of
Aristotle 1–8, 15–17
  as logician 3–4